Leeches

by L. Patricia Kite

Lerner Publications Company • Minneapolis

To curious children everywhere.
                    —*LPK*

Photographs are reproduced with the permission of the following sources: © Todd Strand/Independent Picture Service, cover, pp. 15, 33; © Dr. Y. Lanceau Jacana/Photo Researchers, Inc., p. 4; © Brian Rogers/Visuals Unlimited, p. 5; © Robert and Linda Mitchell, pp. 6, 7, 14, 20, 22, 23, 24, 28, 32, 39, 46–47; © James P. Rowan, pp. 8, 31; © Michael P. Gadomski/Photo Researchers, Inc., p. 9 (top); © Valerie Giles/Photo Researchers, Inc., p. 9 (inset); © Jim Nachel/Root Resources, pp. 10 (both), 11; © L. Newman & A. Flowers/Photo Researchers, Inc., pp. 12, 26; © James H. Robinson/Photo Researchers, Inc., p. 13 (top); © Oliver Meckes/Photo Researchers, Inc., pp. 13 (bottom), 25; © Gregory G. Dimijian/Photo Researchers, Inc., p. 16; © Jeff Lepore/Photo Researchers, Inc., p. 17; © Steve Austin/Papilio/ CORBIS, p. 18; © Scott Camazine/Photo Researchers, Inc., p. 19; © Tim Davis/Photo Researchers, Inc., p. 21; © Martin Dohrn/SPL/Photo Researchers, Inc., p. 27; © Wayne Lawler/ Photo Researchers, Inc., pp. 29, 30; © Science VU/Visuals Unlimited, p. 34; © Jen and Des Bartlett/Bruce Coleman, Inc., p. 35; © Bob Gossington/Bruce Coleman, Inc., p. 36; © Janis Burger/Bruce Coleman, Inc., p. 37; © Jean-Loup Charmet/SPL/Photo Researchers, Inc., p. 38; © St. Bartholomew's Hospital/SPL/Photo Researchers, Inc., p. 40; © Pascal Goetgheluck/SPL/ Photo Researchers, Inc., p. 41; © Astrid & Hanns-Frieder Michler/SPL/Photo Researchers, Inc., p. 42; © A. B. Sheldon/Root Resources, p. 43.

Lerner Publications Company
A division of Lerner Publishing Group
241 First Avenue North
Minneapolis, Minnesota 55401 U.S.A.

Website address: www.lernerbooks.com

Library of Congress Cataloging-in-Publication Data

Kite, L. Patricia.
    Leeches / by L. Patricia Kite.
      p.   cm. — (Early bird nature books)
    Summary: Describes the different species of leeches, their
  physical characteristics, behavior, and life cycle.
    Includes index.
    ISBN: 0–8225–3054–6 (lib. bdg. : alk. paper)
    1. Leeches—Juvenile literature. [1. Leeches.] I. Title.
  II. Series.
  QL391.A6K49 2005
  592'.66—dc22   2003017852

Manufactured in the United States of America
1 2 3 4 5 6 – JR – 10 09 08 07 06 05

Contents

Be a Word Detective

Can you find these words as you read about the leech's life? Be a detective and try to figure out what they mean. You can turn to the glossary on page 46 for help.

anesthetic   **cocoon**   **saliva**

annelids   **hosts**   **segments**

anticoagulant   **parasitic**

clotting   **proboscis**

Chapter 1

A leech sucks blood. Leeches live in many places. What kinds of places do leeches like to live?

Leech Life

Some leeches suck the blood of people and animals. These leeches are the ones most people have heard about. But there are other kinds of leeches. These leeches eat other kinds of food.

There are at least 650 species, or kinds, of leeches. They live all over the world. All leeches live in places that are wet or damp.

Leeches live in wet, damp places all over the world.

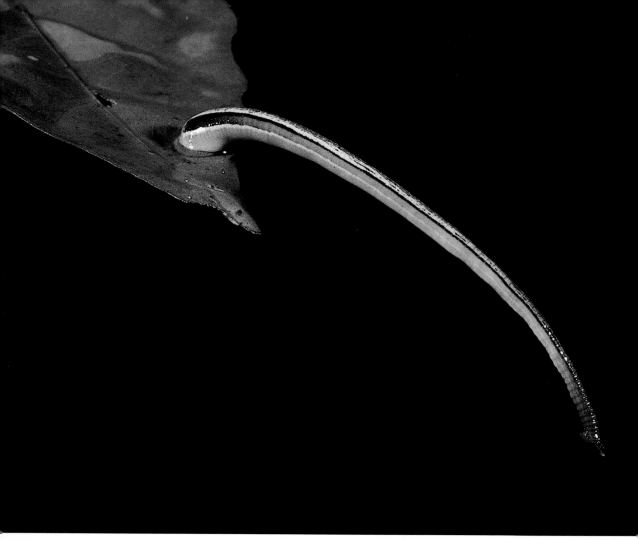

Some leeches live on land near water.

Most species of leeches live in lakes, ponds, swamps, or streams. Some species of leeches live in the ocean. A few species live on land. Most land leeches live in damp, warm parts of the world.

Leeches are related to earthworms (top). *Leeches and earthworms have similar bodies* (inset).

Leeches are related to earthworms. Leeches and earthworms belong to a group of animals called annelids (AN-eh-lihdz). Annelids are worms that have segments (SEHG-mehntz). Segments are parts shaped like rings along a worm's body.

Leeches have 34 segments. Segments help leeches to change the shape of their body. Sometimes leeches are short and wide. And sometimes leeches stretch out. Then they are long and thin.

Leeches can be short and wide (top). *They can also become long and thin* (bottom).

This leech is black. Are all leeches black?

Leeches come in many sizes. Most are 1 to 8 inches long when they are stretched out. The smallest leeches are about ¼ inch long. This is about as long as the fingernail on your little finger. The largest species is about 18 inches long when it is stretched out. This is about as long as your arm!

Many leeches are black, gray, brown, or olive green. But some are very colorful. They may have red, black, orange, or yellow spots. Or they may have yellow, red, or black stripes.

Some leeches have spots or stripes.

Leeches have two suckers (top). *This is a close-up view of a leech's sucker* (bottom).

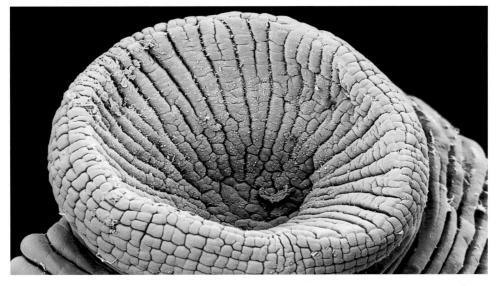

All leeches have two suckers. The smaller sucker is on the front end of the leech's body. This sucker is where the leech's mouth is. The larger sucker is on the back end of the leech's body. This sucker helps the leech hold on to surfaces such as soil, rocks, or animals.

Leeches use their suckers to move.

Leeches use both suckers to move along a surface. First, a leech stretches out. It sticks its front sucker to a surface. Then it places its back sucker near the front sucker. The leech's body looks like a loop. Then the leech stretches the front sucker forward and sticks it to the surface. The leech loops over and over again to travel. A leech can move quite quickly this way.

Many leeches also travel by swimming.
They swim by moving their body up and down.
They look like a wavy line.

Leeches are good swimmers.

Chapter 2

This leech is sucking blood. What are some animals that leeches suck blood from?

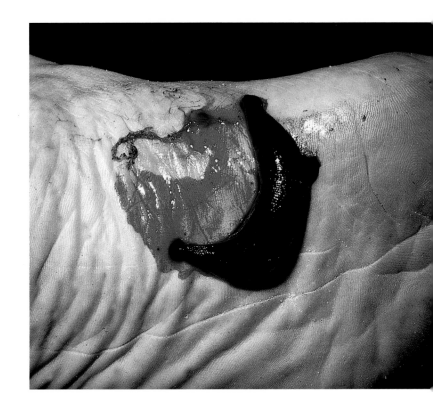

Blood, Anyone?

Many species of leeches are parasitic (PAR-uh-SIT-ik). Parasitic leeches stick themselves to the bodies of other animals. These animals are called hosts. Parasitic leeches eat by sucking blood from their hosts.

Some parasitic leeches feed on only one kind of animal. Others feed on many different kinds of animals. Leeches can feed on the blood of fish, turtles, frogs, birds, rabbits, dogs, and other animals. Leeches can feed on humans too.

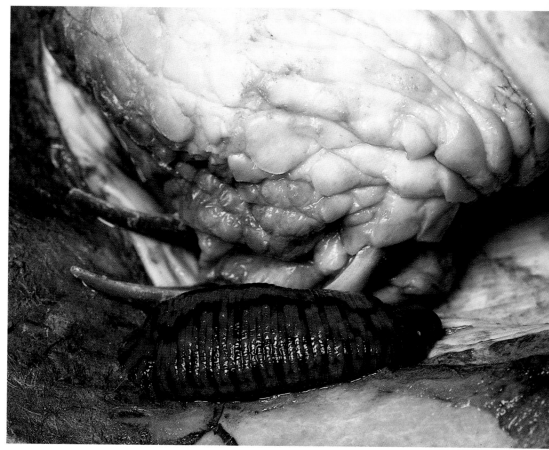

Leeches feed on many different animals. This leech is sucking blood from a turtle.

Different kinds of leeches eat different kinds of food.
This leech is eating a worm.

Some species of leeches are not parasitic. They do not suck blood. These leeches eat young insects, fish eggs, small worms, snails, slugs, and even other leeches. Or they eat tiny animals or plants that live in the water. Some leeches eat plants and animals that are dead and rotting.

There are also leeches that sometimes suck blood. But at other times they eat animals and plants.

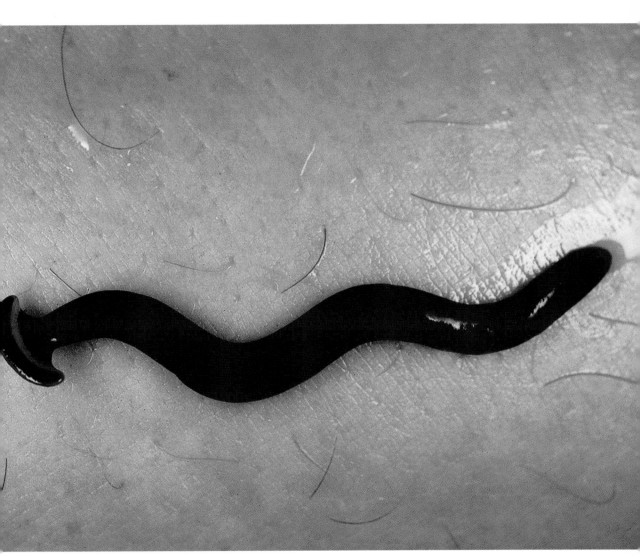

Sometimes leeches suck blood from humans.

Chapter 3

Leeches search for food. What senses do leeches use to find food?

Finding Food

A leech stretches itself out when it is hungry. It tries to sense if food is nearby. It may stay very still in the water or on land. Or it may wave its head and body around to sense food.

Leeches have two or more eyes on their head. Their eyes can sense a change in light. A change in light could mean that food is nearby. Many leeches also have other parts on their body that can sense a change in light.

Leeches stretch out when they search for food. They get long and thin.

Leeches also have special body parts that help them find food. Parts on a leech's head can sense smells. Special parts on its body can feel a change in heat or cold. Warmer water or air could mean that food is nearby.

Leeches can feel changes in temperature.

Leeches can feel changes in how water or air moves around them. This helps leeches tell if an animal is moving near them. If a leech senses that food is nearby, the leech swims or crawls toward the food.

Leeches can sense animals moving around them.

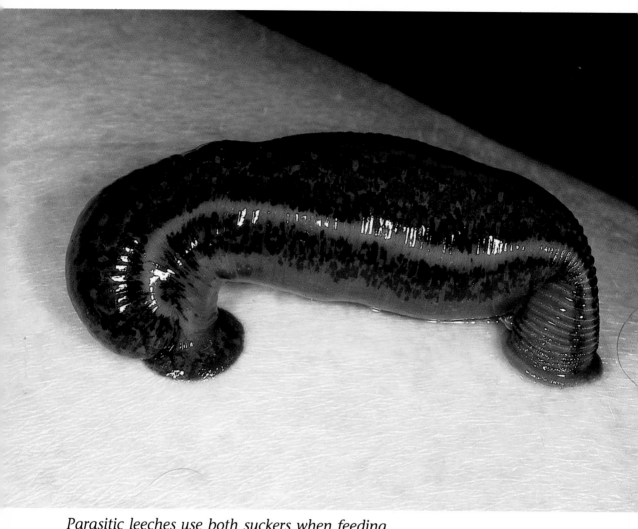

Parasitic leeches use both suckers when feeding.

Parasitic leeches stick themselves to a host. First, they put their back sucker on the host to hold on. Then they place their front sucker. The leech can begin to feed.

24

Some parasitic leeches have jaws with many teeth. The teeth are like little saws. They cut through the host's skin. Then the leech sucks the host's blood. The leech's bite leaves a mark that looks like the letter *Y*.

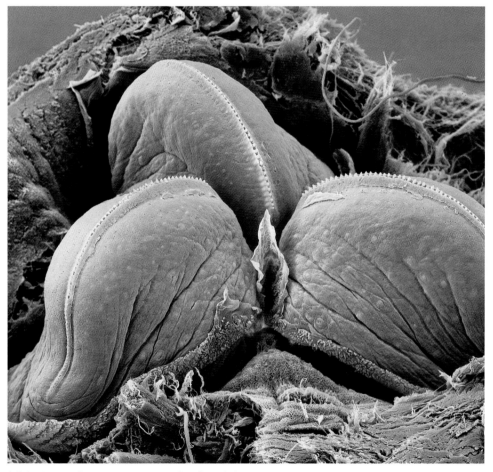

This is a close-up view of a leech's jaws.

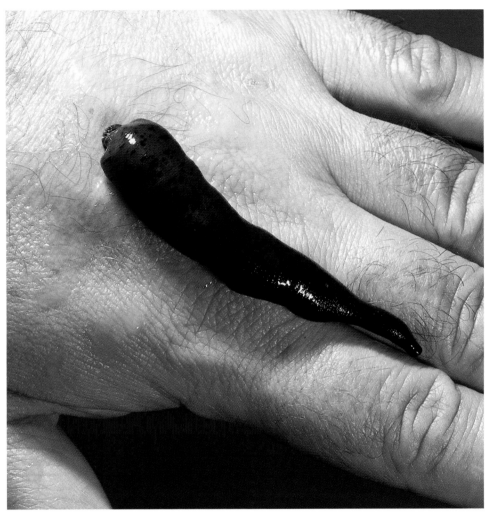

Some leeches do not have jaws.

Other parasitic leeches have a proboscis
(pruh-BAH-suhs) instead of jaws. A proboscis
looks like a needle. A leech sticks its proboscis
into a host. Then it sucks out the host's blood.

A leech is thick after a big meal.

Parasitic leeches eat a lot at one time. They can eat over five times as much as they weigh. A leech that is very small can become as big as a thick marker.

Leeches eat as much as they can when they get a chance to feed.

Parasitic leeches make special saliva (suh-LYE-vuh), or spit, in their mouths. Leeches' saliva helps them eat a lot at one time. Leeches spread their saliva onto areas where they feed. The saliva has an anesthetic (AN-ehs-THE-tik) in it. An anesthetic stops pain. It keeps the host from feeling the bite of the leech. The host may not notice the leech for many hours.

A person might not notice a feeding leech.

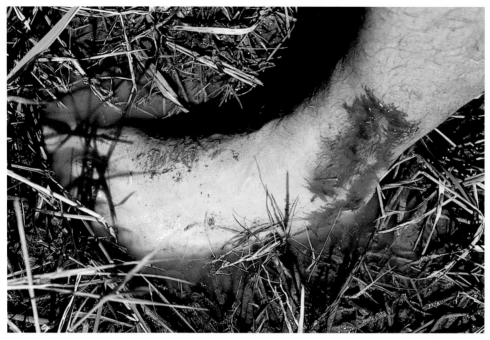

A leech's saliva helps keep blood flowing.

When an animal's skin is cut, blood flows.
Usually it flows for only a short time. Then the
blood clots. It becomes thick and makes a scab.
But leeches have a way to keep blood from
clotting (KLAHT-ing). A leech's saliva has an
anticoagulant (AN-tye-koh-AG-yoo-lehnt) in it.
Anticoagulants stop blood from clotting. The
host's blood keeps flowing. So the leech can
keep feeding for a long time.

30

When it is full, the leech falls off of its host. The leech will be able to wait for many months before it needs to eat again.

A full leech will not have to eat again for a long time.

Chapter 4

Leeches lay many eggs at one time. But being a young leech is dangerous. What dangers do young leeches face?

Baby Leeches

Leeches hatch from eggs. Most species of leeches lay eggs in late spring. They lay up to three hundred eggs at a time. Each species lays a different number of eggs.

Most leeches lay their eggs in a cocoon (kuh-KOON). A cocoon is a safe shelter. Leeches make their cocoon with their body.

Some species of leeches bury their cocoons in mud or damp soil. Other species put their cocoons on a rock, plant, or log. Usually the adult leeches go away after laying eggs. The baby leeches hatch from their eggs a few weeks or months later. The babies must find their own food.

Leeches put their cocoons in safe places. Rocks and plants are good places for cocoons.

Most leeches leave after laying eggs. Some leeches stay with their eggs.

But some adults do not leave their eggs. Some adults stay near their cocoons until the eggs hatch. Other adults keep their cocoons on their bellies. The cocoon may stay on the parent for several weeks or months. It stays until the eggs hatch. Sometimes these babies stick themselves to their parents' bellies.

34

If a baby falls off, its parent may try to help it climb back on. Adult leeches may curl around their babies to protect them from enemies. Some animals hunt and eat leeches. Fish, turtles, and some birds eat leeches. And some large leeches eat smaller leeches.

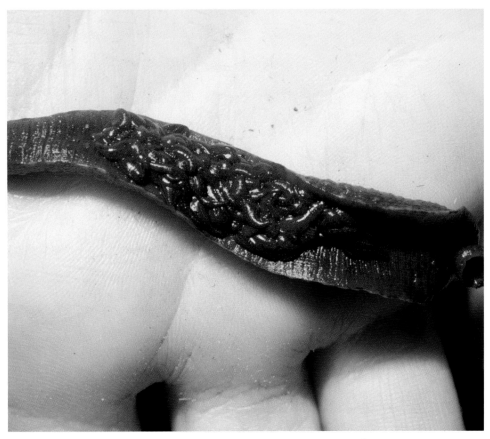

Some adult leeches protect their young by carrying them.

The baby leeches may stay attached, or stuck, to their parent for several weeks or months. They eat whatever their parent eats. Then the babies are ready to live on their own.

Some young leeches depend on their parent for food. Others must find their own food.

Young leeches need food to grow.

Every time a baby leech eats, it grows. A baby leech needs to eat about four meals before it becomes an adult. Then it can lay its own eggs. Most species of leeches live for 2 to 6 years. But some species live up to 20 years.

Chapter 5

People have used leeches to heal the sick for many years.

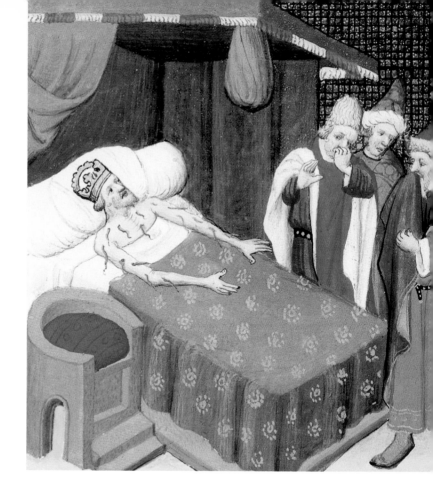

People and Leeches

People have used leeches as a treatment for illness for over two thousand years. People once believed that illness was caused by bad blood. They thought leeches sucked out bad blood and cured illness. Early doctors put leeches on the sick. They let leeches feed, but this did not make people well. For a while, doctors stopped using leeches.

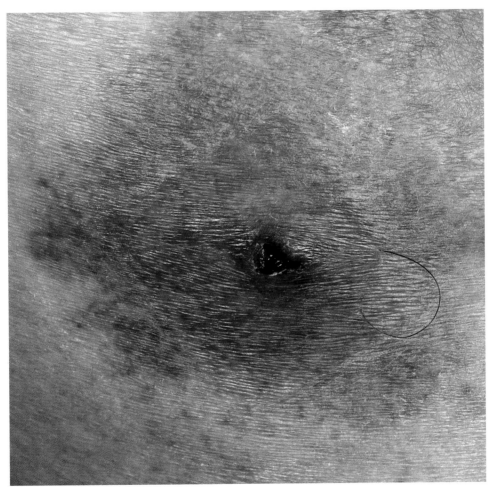

Leeches can cause too much bleeding. Doctors try to keep this from happening.

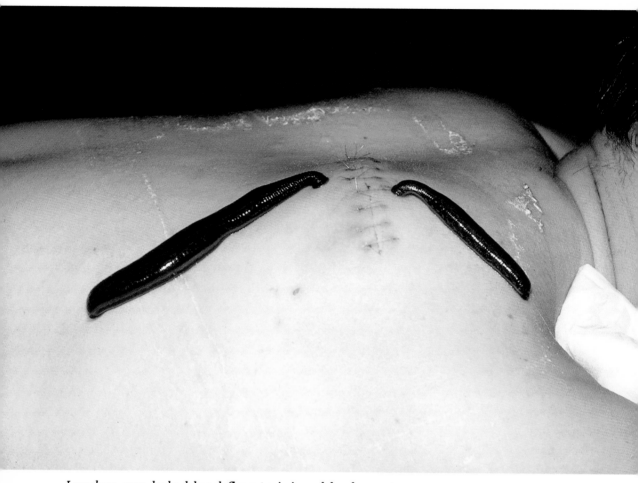

Leeches can help blood flow to injured body parts.

Then, not long ago, doctors began using a type of leech in hospitals. These leeches are used in ways that really can help. Doctors sometimes put leeches on people who have had an operation. The leeches feed on a spot near

where the operation was done. The leeches'
anticoagulant stops the blood from clotting
right away. The blood keeps flowing to the spot
as it should. Then the person can heal faster.

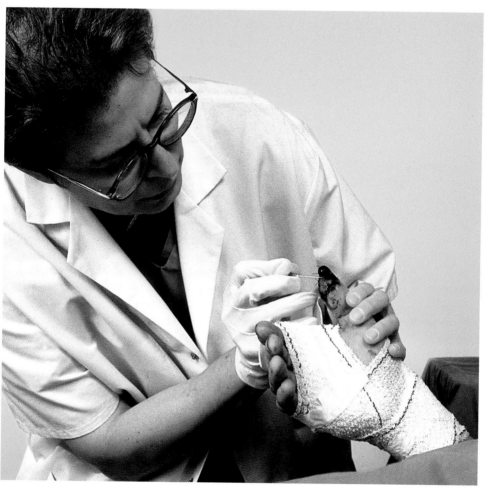

*A steady flow of blood can help injured body parts heal
more quickly.*

Leech saliva might someday help people with heart problems.

Doctors are trying to find other ways to use leech saliva to help people who are ill. Someday leech saliva may help people who have had heart attacks.

Leeches are interesting animals. Look for one next time you are in a wet or damp area. It may already sense that you are nearby.

People and leeches have an interesting relationship.

On Sharing a Book

As you know, adults greatly influence a child's attitude toward reading. When a child sees you read, or when you share a book with a child, you're sending a message that reading is important. Show the child that reading a book together is important to you. Find a comfortable, quiet place. Turn off the television and limit other distractions, such as telephone calls.

Be prepared to start slowly. Take turns reading parts of this book. Stop and talk about what you're reading. Talk about the photographs. You may find that much of the shared time is spent discussing just a few pages. This discussion time is valuable for both of you, so don't move through the book too quickly. If the child begins to lose interest, stop reading. Continue sharing the book at another time. When you do pick up the book again, be sure to revisit the parts you have already read. Most importantly, enjoy the book!

Be a Vocabulary Detective

You will find a word list on page 5. Words selected for this list are important to the understanding of the topic of this book. Encourage the child to be a word detective and search for the words as you read the book together. Talk about what the words mean and how they are used in the sentence. Do any of these words have more than one meaning? You will find these words defined in a glossary on page 46.

What about Questions?

Use questions to make sure the child understands the information in this book. Here are some suggestions:

> What did this paragraph tell us? What does this picture show? What do you think we'll learn about next? What kind of animal is a leech? How many species of leeches are there? Where do leeches live? How do leeches move? What do leeches eat? How do leeches find food? How do leeches eat? What animals are dangerous to leeches? What did people use leeches for long ago? How do people use leeches in modern times? What is your favorite part of this book? Why?

If the child has questions, don't hesitate to respond with questions of your own, such as What do *you* think? Why? What is it that you don't know? If the child can't remember certain facts, turn to the index.

Introducing the Index

The index is an important learning tool. It helps readers get information quickly without searching throughout the whole book. Turn to the index on page 47. Choose an entry, such as *food* and ask the child to use the index to find out what foods leeches eat. Repeat this exercise with as many entries as you like. Ask the child to point out the differences between an index and a glossary. (The index helps readers find information quickly, while the glossary tells readers what words mean.)

Where in the World?

Many plants and animals found in the Early Bird Nature Books series live in parts of the world other than the United States. Encourage the child to find places where leeches live on a world map or globe. Take time to talk about climate, terrain, and how you might live in such places.

All the World in Metric!

Although our monetary system is in metric units (based on multiples of 10), the United States is one of the few countries in the world that does not use the metric system of measurement. Here are some conversion activities you and the child can do using a calculator:

WHEN YOU KNOW:	MULTIPLY BY:	TO FIND:
miles	1.609	kilometers
feet	0.3048	meters
inches	2.54	centimeters
gallons	3.785	liters
tons	0.907	metric tons
pounds	0.454	kilograms

Activities

Make up a story about a leech. Be sure to include information from this book. Draw or paint pictures to illustrate your story.

Visit a nearby lake, pond, or swamp in the summertime and look for leeches in the shallow parts. What color are they? What do they look like when they swim? Do they move toward you?

Glossary

anesthetic (AN-ehs-THE-tik): a part of a leech's spit that stops pain

annelids (AN-eh-lihdz): worms whose bodies are in segments

anticoagulant (AN-tye-koh-AG-yoo-lehnt): a part of leeches' spit that keeps blood flowing

clotting (KLAHT-ing): when blood becomes thick and stops flowing

cocoon (kuh-KOON): a safe shelter for leech eggs

hosts: animals from which leeches suck blood

parasitic (PAR-uh-SIT-ik): living on another animal and getting food from it

proboscis (pruh-BAHS-uhs): a narrow needle-like body part that some leeches use to suck blood

saliva (suh-LYE-vuh): spit

segments (SEHG-mehntz): parts shaped like rings along a leech's body

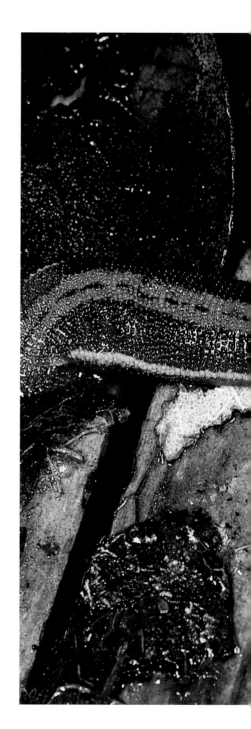

Index

About the Author

L. Patricia "Pat" Kite used to think leeches were "yucky." But her children really enjoyed studying the leeches living in a friend's pond. "Do a book about them," they urged. The more Kite learned about leeches, the more interested she became. So here is the book, dedicated to curious children everywhere. Kite has a bachelor of science degree from the University of California Medical Center, San Francisco, California. She also holds teaching credentials in biology and social science and a master's degree in journalism. Her prior books include *Raccoons* and *Cockroaches.*